Psychology

How To Analyze People Using Human Psychological Techniques, Body Language Signals, Social Skills And Personality Types

LELA GIBSON

CONTENTS

Introduction

I want to thank you and congratulate you for buying the book, *"Psychology: How To Analyze People Using Human Psychological Techniques, Body Language Signals, Social Skills And Personality Types"*.

This book has actionable information on how to analyze people using human psychological techniques, body language signals, social skills and personality types.

"If only I could know what he/she is thinking…?" This statement is one most of us have used at one time or the other. Let us not forget the common regret statement of, *"how could I not see X for what he/she truly is? How could I be so blind?"*

Many are the times when we wish we had the ability to read the mind of those we are in love with, those we do business with, and those we associate with on an everyday basis. This wish, although nothing but a wish, comes from the fact that knowing what someone is thinking would make communicating and relating infinitely easy.

If we could read minds, we would know what to do or say at the right time. We would never have to worry about how others perceive you, and we would not have to waste so much time on people who did not deserve it. If we could read minds, the world would be 'sucker' free. Such ability would save so much time and trouble!

While the ability to read minds may seem like something out of a Sci-Fi movie, did you know that if you applied psychology to analyze people, you could actually 'read them like a book'? A person is a series of behaviors and verbal and non-verbal symbols that if you learn how to analyze, you can gain a supernatural ability: reading people and knowing what they are thinking.

From this amazing book, you are going to learn how to use psychological techniques, personality types, and body language signals to read people as you would an open book. Let's begin.

Thanks again for buying this book. I hope you enjoy it!

Let's start by building an understanding of human psychology before we learn how to 'read' people like open books.

Understanding Human Psychology

Humans are natural social beings: our survival depends on interacting with one another. However, knowing whom you are talking to, how to talk to him/her as well as understanding their intentions is very critical if you are to understand and analyze their human psychology.

Psychology normally concerns itself with human behavior; it explains why people behave as they do. In the same light, you should note that behavior does not limit itself to what we do; it also touches on what we think and what we feel. Psychology seeks to interpret our physical responses as well as our mental ones.

To know what someone is thinking, or whom a person is (their interests, dislikes), you could ask the person, or if that is out of the question, give the person a self-assessment test.

Unfortunately, people are not always straightforward, and as such, although the above approach could work, it has limitations. For one, many people very reluctantly voice what they are truly feeling or thinking not because they are trying to be crafty, but because it is human nature to desire to reflect the 'right emotions/thoughts/words' or the least embarrassing ones.

When you understand human psychology, you learn how to read people so you can understand what they are thinking but not saying; you learn to watch people for clues about who they really are.

To understand the visible behavior you or others display, let us take a behind-the-scenes look human mind processing:

The Psychology of a Human Mind

Psychologists view the human brain as a kind of computer. It takes in information (input), processes and stores it in various ways, and then produces an output (visible behavior).

This means:

1. How we react to the world, our behavior/reaction starts with a sensory perception i.e. the way your five main senses along with other sensory abilities input information to your brain.

2. The second step is processing and storage. In this part, the brain/mind works through the data from the sensory perception, and tries to 'make sense of it'. The important information is committed to memory, which is why you will remember something that you have seen, smelt, felt, or heard.

3. The third step is releasing the output, which is the display of visible behavior for example a frown, wrinkling of the nose, a touch, a smirk, and so on.

These three steps show us that every reaction and emotion has a trigger that lays in our senses. When trying to understand why people do the things they do, it is important to consider the trigger: it connects us to the behavior and makes it easier to understand why.

Each of us processes information differently. Even when exposed to similar experiences, our senses will pick it up in a similar manner, but the experience will be different through the processing such that the output varies from one person to the next. Why is this so? Psychology has tried to find out.

It is the reason why we can barely understand our own behavior (most times) and why it is so hard to understand others' behavior. Charles dickens once pointed out:

"A wonderful fact to reflect upon, that every human creature is constituted to be that profound secret and mystery to every other."

Thanks to psychology, these 'mystery' are now solvable. You can read and understand others; they call it 'read people like a book'. Lets learn how in the following chapters.

Using Psychological Techniques to Analyze People

When reading people, you should always keep in mind that there is always 'more than meets the eye' and more than said. For instance, you may meet a casually dressed man who introduces himself as a retail store owner but in the real sense, he is spy (these ones are very good at camouflage). Would you, in your infinite wisdom, know if that man is a spy? Yes, you would, but only if you paid attention to the person's verbal and non-verbal cues, manner of talking, keenness on things that are not as intriguing, among others.

Analyzing someone demands that you observe and interpret that person's verbal and non-verbal cues, even the ones you think are insignificant: the ones that are easy to miss, the ones that allow you to see past the person's masks and into the real person.

You see, logic alone cannot tell you the whole story; enough people know how to just enough information to manipulate you into thinking of them a certain way. For this reason alone, you ought to seek other vital forms of information so you can learn to read the intuitive cues people give off.

Other than being a keen observer (without ogling), you also need to let go of preconceptions and emotions that may distort information about a person: they act as translucent objects that prevent you from seeing a person clearly, for who they are.

For instance, if you had a disagreement with someone a year ago and you are still carrying the emotional baggage, a smile may mean mockery instead of a kind gesture. This is why to avoid misinterpretation and distortion, you must remain objective and receive information neutrally; it also means you should surrender all biases and let go of limiting ideas.

Let us explore the three basic techniques used in the art of reading people;

1st: Observe Body Cues

Words account for a very small percentage (about 7%) of how we communicate. Body language accounts for a bigger percentage (55%) while voice tone and intonation account for the remaining 30%. This shows that body language will tell you more than half about a person.

Reading non-verbal cues calls for relaxation and fluidity; do not try too hard to read body language cues. Desist from being too intense and analytical as you may end up being paranoid or making the other person conscious of your 'observation.'

Below are the common cues you should look out for:

Appearance (Analyzing the Cover)

How does the person appear? Below are a few suggestions of things about appearance you should pay attention to:

What is the person wearing?

Identify a piece of clothing that may help you identify a person's occupation for instance a lab coat, tool belt, a power suit, or a uniform. This could help you identify what a person does professionally. A power suit and well-shined shoes indicate ambition and a person dressed for success. A person dressed in this manner likely holds a prominent work designation or such a person is sure he or she is on his or her way to an important position.

Jeans and a t-shirt may indicate comfort with being casual while a tight top with cleavage may communicate seduction.

How does the skin look?

Is the skin wrinkly, rough, normal, or does the person have exceptional petal soft skin? Lines near the neck, mouth or the eyes will tell you how old a person is likely to be; this will guide you on how to talk and what to talk about (generally how to behave) as it should be things that could spark their interest.

The skin could also tell you where a person is from and the person's health status since most of the time, the nature of the skin is a reflection of internal health and the environment one lives in on a day-to-day basis. For instance, smokers and people often exposed to sun are more likely to have dull and wrinkled skin.

Can you spot affluence?

People show wealth or the desire to be wealthy in the quality of garments, shoes, or accessories they wear. However, when it comes to spotting affluence, be careful because many educated and wealthy individuals such as Mark Zuckerberg and Bill Gates prefer casual clothing.

Instead of looking for designers clothing, look for signs of thriftiness. For instance, faded clothing, worn shoes and discount clothing labels may indicate (though not necessarily) that a person has less money.

All the signals mentioned above may tell you the economic decisions a person has made; however, these rarely (if ever) translate into behavior.

Do you notice fastidiousness?

A person who has his or her hair in place, tie neatly tied, and clothing pressed, someone who pays attention to every detail of his or her clothing may indicate that a person is very detail oriented while a disheveled person may be creative or messy.

How is the posture?

Have you ever met someone who took charge of the room the moment they entered it? If yes, that effect is mainly because of their body language. Your body comprises of your posture, gestures and eye contact. If someone has a high power body language which comprises of keeping the body straight, limbs open, maintaining direct eye contact and walking with confidence, he/ she is likely to be extremely strong and confident and is likely to influence people easily. However, if someone slouches when walking or sitting, keeps his/ her limbs closed, does not look their listeners in the eyes and maintains a timid posture, he/ she is likely to have a low power body language and is quite likely to lack confidence. That person is also likely to feel intimidated by others and will have trouble expressing his/ her viewpoints to others.

When you are in a room, observe those around you closely. Does the person hold his or her head high as a sign of confidence or does he or she cower or walk indecisively as a sign of low self-esteem? If a person walks with swagger and a puffed out chest, it could be an indication of a big ego/pride.

Physical Movements

Has the person crossed his or her arms and legs? This could indicate defensiveness, self-protection, aloofness, or anger. When a person crosses his or her legs, that person points his/her toes (of the top leg) towards the person he or she is more at ease with.

Is the person picking cuticles or biting his/her lips? If so, that person may be in an awkward situation, under pressure or trying to soothe him/herself.

Facial Expressions

Emotions etch themselves on our faces no matter how hard we may try to hide them. In this regard, look out for the following:

2nd: Listen To Your Intuition

It is possible to use your intuition to tune into someone beyond his or her body language and words. Your intuition refers to what the gut feels and not what your head thinks; intuition is that inner voice telling you to do or not do something. It does not rely on logic; it is more about the body knowing: your body just knows. Intuitions tunes into who the person is rather than the person's outer trappings. It lets you see further than the obvious.

Here are intuitive cues you can monitor:

Gut feeling

A gut feeling is a visceral reaction, which normally occurs before you can even have the chance to think (before your mind develops an opinion). It relays whether you are at ease or not; a gut feeling is your internal truth meter that tells you whether people deserve your trust or not- listen to it.

Goose bumps

Goose bumps are intuitive tingles that convey our connection with people who move or inspire us or who say something we resonate with. They also happen during a déjà-vu moment, which is when you meet someone/or see something you feel you recognize although you may have never met before.

Intuitive empathy

Sometimes you can experience other people's physical symptoms on your body in what experts now regard as an intense form of empathy. After a meeting with someone, does your head hurt when it previously did not? Are you upset? If so, you will need to get feedback from the individual you met (ask how that person is) to determine whether what you are experiencing is empathy.

3rd: Sensing Emotional Energy

Our emotions express our energy, the energy we give off otherwise called 'vibes.' Vibes register not in the mind but intuitively; a vibe is an invisible energy felt a few inches from the body.

People with good vibes feel good to be around. In fact, they usually improve your mood and vitality such that you want to stay with them longer. On the other hand, when around those with a negative vibe, you feel drained and instinctively, you want to get away.

Cues for reading emotional energy

Sense their presence

'Presence' represents the overall energy we emit and that does not relate to words or behavior. Presence is more like an energy field that surrounds us like a halo. Notice this energy around a person; it can either attract you or repel you. If it gives you the creeps, you may need to be careful.

Watch the eyes

Have you ever looked at a person's eyes and thought you saw something dark and evil there? If you stayed, you probably discovered something weird about the person. This is because our eyes transmit powerful energies.

Observe the eyes

Are they tranquil, caring, sexy, angry, or mean? Do they seem guarded or deceptive? You can also observe a person's eyes to determine if there is a capacity for intimacy with someone: if there is someone at home in their eyes.

Listen for tone of voice or laugh

The tone of our voices can tell volumes about our emotions. This is perhaps because sound frequencies usually create vibrations, which transmit either negative or positive energy. Notice how someone's tone of voice affects you. Does it feel soothing, snippy, or whiny?

Notice the feel of physical contact: a handshake, hug, or touch

As humans, we have the ability to share emotional energy through our physical contact like an electrical current. Does a handshake feel limp suggesting timidity or being non-committal? Does it feel warm, comforting, or confident, or does it make you uncomfortable to a point where you want to withdraw?

If you pay attention to these psychological cues, you will be in a position to read and understand people even before they utter a word.

To learn more about analyzing specific body language cues, head to the next chapter:

Analyzing Specific Body Language Signals

Other than common gestures such fidgeting and leg crossing, we (humans) send body signals through specific body parts such as the eyes.

In this chapter, we shall have a deep discussion about body signals and learn how to notice them and decipher their true meaning. Note that it is easy to miss or misinterpret body language cues and therefore, you ought to be keen and unbiased.

1: Eye Reading

Eyes are very vital organs that allow us to see the beauty around us. Did you know that other than giving you the gift of sight, the eyes give away your emotions? In fact, many of us consider the eyes 'windows to the soul' and just by gazing into them, you can learn a lot about a person.

The beauty of reading eye signals is that you will seldom be wrong: there is no way to distort signals from the eyes (especially the pupil) because we cannot control the size of our pupils.

Here are the various eye reading cues that shall help you read people:

1: The Pupils

As mentioned earlier, we cannot control our pupils. In the process of sight, they adjust the amount of light taken in by the eyes; they dilate (size increasing) or contract (size decreasing).

In a research study conducted by Eckhard Hess (1975), he found out that the pupil also dilates when we are interested in a person we are talking to, an object we are looking at, or a subject we are talking about. Whenever something is less interesting, the pupils will contract.

The next time you are talking to someone, watch the person's eyes (but do not stare) and notice the variations—you may vary interesting and non-interesting topics just to notice the change in the pupils.

2: *Eye Contact*

Effective eye contact is crucial to effective communication. However, as many cultures dictate, eye contact should be regular, not constant.

Persistent eye contact is an attempt at intimidation

Persistent eye contact makes someone feel overly studied and may make lead to discomfort. This is why if you are reading someone's eyes, you should not persistently look into the person's eyes.

When other people are making persistent eye contact, it may mean they are over-aware of the messages they are emitting. In addition, a person who is being deceptive will try to distort eye contact so that he or she is neither making it nor avoiding it.

Evasive Eye Contact

This could be a sign of discomfort, shame, dishonesty, or deception. Moreover, it could be that a person is focusing on perceptive tasks or calculating to come up with an answer especially when a person has to think hard about something.

3: *Blinking*

Our eyes instinctively blink. However, our emotions and feelings can cause a subconscious alteration of our blink rate: like the pupils, this is something we have no control over. Blinking more than the average 6-10 times a minute could be an indicator of nervousness or attraction to the person you are talking to (it is a sign of flirting).

4: Eye Direction

Normally, the direction someone is looking at tells us what someone is looking at. However, the direction of someone's eyes can give you an insight into what the person is thinking.

Looking to the right indicates the person is having creative thoughts while looking to the left indicates someone trying to remember something. The latter could be a potential sign of lying: someone trying to create a version of events.

Moreover, pay attention to how the other person looks at you to figure out whether or not they are honest about what they are saying. It is believed that if someone is unable to look you directly in the eye, he/ she is presumably lying. This is based on the assumption that is difficult to maintain your gaze when you are lying to someone. However, many of us overcompensate at times and maintain eye contact to the extent that it feels strange. On average, an American maintains eye contact for about 7 to 10 seconds. This timespan increases when you are listening to someone. If you are in conversation with someone who is constantly staring at you and his/ her gaze is making you feel weird particularly if he/ she is not blinking and is very still, it is likely that he/ she may be up to something and are not honest to you.

5: Eyebrows

Raised eyebrows could be an indication of fear, worry, or surprise. It usually conveys discomfort. The next time someone compliments your dress with his or her eyebrows raised, you should be concerned because that person is being insincere.

6: Exaggerated nodding

To show approval, a person only needs to nod not more than twice. When you tell someone something and the person nods excessively, it is an indication that the person is anxious or worried about your opinion of him or her, or that you doubt the person's ability to follow through with the instructions.

7: *Real Smile versus Fake Smile*

A smile indicates happiness or pleasure. However not all smiles do: some are fake and deceptive. The good or bad thing (depending on the whether you are on the receiving or giving end) is that when it comes to a smile, the mouth can lie but the eyes will not.

Genuine smiles usually reach the eyes. They crinkle the skin at the corners of your eyes to create what they call 'crow's feet' around the eyes. A genuine smile reflects from the eyes.

In a case where the smile is only on the lips while the eyes remain unchanged, this is a fake smile: watch out. People tend to smile to hide some of what they are thinking or feeling and as is often the case, what they are feeling or thinking is not pleasant.

If you suspect someone is lying, observe their eyes when they smile. Genuine smiles that come right from within reach your eyes and crinkle your skin at the ends to create creases like crow's feet at the edges of your eyes. Quite often, people smile or grin when they wish to hide their feelings and emotions. If you think someone is concealing the truth and not being completely honest about their feelings, observe the corners of their eyes. If you don't see any creases at the ends, it is likely they are hiding something behind their smile.

8: *Mirroring Body Language*

When talking to someone, does he or she smile when you do or lean his or her head the same way as yours? This is what we call mirroring body language. It is something we usually do unconsciously whenever we feel a bond with a person. When this happens, it means a conversation is going well and the other person is interested and is receptive to your ideas. It is a good sign that you are winning the person over.

9: Voice Features

Voice features can help us decipher Para verbal communication (supported by the limbic part of the brain). Here are the various voice features you should pay attention to as you seek to become a people-reading master:

Tone

Increased tones express safety while decreased tone/inflections indicate insecurity.

Speech speed

Speech can either be slow (250 syllable per min), normal (about 300 syllables per minute), or fast (500 syllables per minute). Fast speech could be an indication of a disorganized speaker who is unsure of what he or she is discussing. In addition, fast speech may indicate that the speaker may be nervous or uncomfortable speaking, which is why he or she is talking fast: to get words out fast and get over with the discussion.

A normal/average speed expresses safety: the speaker knows what he or she wants to say and understands its importance to the audience and him or herself. On the other hand, a slow pace is an impression of low intelligence or unawareness of the subject.

Voice volume

This spells a speaker's authority and the power of persuasion. Low volumes indicate less authority while high volumes may express a speaker's need to be overpowering and dominating such that it is uncomfortable or unpleasant.

Pauses between words and phrases

These can transmit clues about the speaker's attitude, awareness of the subject, and intentions. Too many pauses could be an indication of unawareness or anxiety.

10: Limb Gestures

Below are the various limb gestures you should pay attention to:

Shoulder shrugs

This is a universal sign of not knowing what is going on. When a person shrugs, it could be that he or she does not know or understand what you are saying. A shrug with exposed palms shows openness or nothing concealed.

Open palms

Western history has always associated this gesture with truth, honesty, allegiance, and submission. Humans also use their palms (usually raised) to show they are not a threat.

Pointed finger with a closed hand

We interpret this as an attempt to display dominance. A speaker may figuratively use it to beat his or her listener/s into submission.

Crossed legs

These are a sign of resistance or a lack of connection. In a negotiation, it is not a good sign. Psychologically, crossed legs are a signal of a person closed off at a mental, physical, and emotional level: the person is less likely to make a settlement in a negotiation. Henry H. Calero and Gerard I. Nierenberg videotaped over 2000 negotiations for their book on the body language topic.

All the parties who crossed their legs during the conversation did not agree with Nierenberg and Calero. So if you are trying to persuade someone to work with you or agree with you on a certain topic, make sure to observe his or her legs and arms. If they are crossed, it is quite likely the other person won't agree with you even if he/ she is smiling with you and seems engaged in the conversation.

A shaking leg

This signals a shaky inside state. According to Susan Whitbourne of the University of Massachusetts, a shaky leg signals irritation, or anxiety and in some cases, both. If you are talking to someone and that person keeps shaking their leg, chances are he/ she is upset with you, nervous about something or is frustrated.

Crossed arms

Like crossed legs, this may signal a closed of person.

11. Mouth Gestures

Observing the mouth of someone can also give you lots of important information about him/ her. If someone has a clenched jaw and has her/ his lips pursed, it is likely he/ she is uncomfortable with something and is feeling stressed. Their mind may be elsewhere or they may not be comfortable with being around you. If that person keeps fidgeting a lot, cuts the conversation short and has a clenched jaw, it is likely he/ she is upset with you. If he seems lost somewhere else and has a tight mouth, he/ she may be bothered about something else and is likely to be lost in thought about that issue.

NOTE

When interpreting body language cues, it is important that you be aware of the context. For instance, pupils may dilate or contract because of changes in room lighting. Further, someone may cross his or her arms because he or she is trying to keep warm or because the chairs do not have armrests. Women also tend to cross their legs when they are wearing certain types of clothing such as short skirts; they do this for comfort.

For these reasons, you need to be aware of the environment before you draw conclusions or change strategy based on these body signals. Gestures have different meanings in different situations.

Learning Social Skills and Discovering Personality (The Art of Understanding People)

As mentioned earlier, humans are social beings: we live by interacting with one another. To interact well, we need to be able to get along with one another so we can create and maintain satisfying and healthy relationships.

Social skills are the skills we use to communicate with each other verbally and non-verbally; being the social creatures we are, we have developed different ways to communicate our messages, thoughts, and feelings with each other.

Developing good social skills helps us be aware of how we communicate with other people and the messages we send; it also equips us with the ability to decode and understand how others communicate. Did you know that sometimes people react to you by mirroring your actions or respond to you according to who you are or what you project?

You see, sometimes we judge people wrongly. For instance, you may think that someone was rude to you or maybe did not listen to you because that person is rude or disrespectful in nature. However, it may be that you were not a good listener or yours speech displayed uncertainty. The only way to avoid such situations is to develop our social skills.

In this chapter, we shall discuss basic social skills you ought to master:

1: Listening Skills

There is something attractive and maybe seductive about knowing someone is listening to you. It can soften even the most impossible person because when someone listens to you keenly, it makes you feel important. Good listening skills include:

1. Referring to other's comments later on for example, *"earlier, you mentioned that..."*

2. Making the 'I am listening noises' such as "uh huh," "really," etc.

3. Physical stillness and maintaining eye contact (not persistent eye contact)

4. Developing interest in the other person, nudge him or her to talk about him or herself, really listening, and genuinely enjoying the conversation.

2: Ability to Stay Calm in Social Situations

When in social situations, staying calm and relaxed will help you communicate effectively and socialize well. If your body language relays nervousness, others will find it difficult to relax around you: you become repelling. Learn to control your emotions and maintain your calm so you can make it easier for you to relate with others. For that, make sure to take a few deep breaths whenever you find yourself feeling frustrated, tensed or nervous. Inhale through your nose to a count of 5 and exhale through your mouth to another count of 5. Take about 10 deep breaths using this technique and in a few moments, you will feel calmer than before.

When you become calmer, you will feel more poised too and it will be easier for you to interact with people comfortably. Naturally, when you socialize better with people, you understand them better.

3: Empathy with Genuine Interest in Other People's Situations

Interest in another person's conversation not only makes you comfortable (especially if you have social anxiety), it also makes the other person feel interesting, which then gives the person the confidence to open up more. You can develop this skill if you stop focusing on yourself and instead focus on what is going on around you and other people: outward focus.

Focus on what the other person is saying and listen to him/her with keen interest. The more attention you pay to his/ her words, the more engaged you are likely to become in his/her conversation. Naturally, when the other person feels your attention, they become more drawn towards you and are likely to open up more to you.

Make sure not to fidget around with your watch, phone or anything else because doing so will exhibit your lack of interest in the conversation which is quite likely to upset the other person making it difficult for him/her to open up to you.

4: Knowing How, When, And How Much to Talk about Yourself

Do not turn-off people by talking about yourself too much or too soon. Small talk is not pleasant if you are rambling on and on about yourself. Start conversations with discussions of subjects not personal to either party. In addition, you can exchange personal views but in a balanced way. This does not mean you should not express your viewpoint. You must express your opinions on topic but make sure not to go into lengthy details with people you just met because chances are, they may not be too interested in your personal stories yet and may feel bored. If someone becomes exhausted by your talk, he/she is quite likely not to engage in a conversation with you again.

5: Look Into People Eyes and Smile

If you talk or listen to someone and you are barely looking at him or her, that person will feel as if you are ignoring, you are not interested in him, or her, or you are untrustworthy: maintain eye contact but do not stare. You can make yourself more attractive by smiling whilst you maintain eye contact. When you smile at the other person, he/ she feels your care and attention and also gets the idea that you like him/ her which is likely to drawn him/ her towards you. Make sure to smile genuinely at people so they actually feel your care.

People Observation

People observation is a social skill that refers to observing peoples' actions. It is a great way to get to know others and improve your communication and social skills. People observation focuses on body movements, facial expressions, language, and way of thinking.

Body language and movement patterns can tell you what people are thinking. To notice them, you have to master the art of observation while still practicing the social skills mentioned above. You have to look without staring, and at the same time, listen keenly so you can make correlations between movements and words.

Here are people observation cues:

Body Movements

Detect particular movements of the body language. Start with mastering movement of the main body parts such as the arms and legs to less noticeable parts such as the eyelashes.

Expressions

These can give you much more information about the inner world of other people though they may be harder to detect. Once you master it, your intuition with others improves, giving you an advantage over others when you interact.

Language

Language will give you an insight on people. It can tell you their personality types. People will use words and they will be able to communicate their attitudes and intentions. You can spot a defensive person or a person with low-self-esteem by the language he or she uses. One of the major languages you ought to look out for in verbal communication is meta-language.

Meta-language

This is a subcomponent of verbal language; it means 'words behind words.' This type of language allows a person to manipulate the perception of others while remaining well mannered.

Let us look at 9 most common meta-words.

1: 'Believe me'

These words, when used before or after a response, announce a lie, no matter how convincing someone tries to make them. The person is trying too hard to convince you.

2: 'But'

When used after an explanation, it may indicate the person was not honest up to that point and contradicts the words they said before.

3: 'I am trying'

It could mean the person is expressing doubts about his or her ability to perform a task. This is common in people who do not usually get things done.

4: 'Only'

Used to minimize the significance of what is to be said.

5: 'Ok' or 'yes'

Used at the end of a sentence, the intent is force the listener to agree with what was said: it is manipulative.

6: 'Honestly' or 'on my honor'

It shows the speaker will most likely not be honest.

7: 'Yes, but'

These are words used to avoid intimidation by simulating agreement.

8: 'Just'

Often used to alleviate guilt or minimize culpability for undesirable consequences.

9: 'I hope for, I wish, I could'

These words are common in people who want to remain neutral when giving opinions. They are a wise way to provide no opinion.

Meta-language communicates volumes. Sadly, most people do not read this language and thus fail to read the deeper meaning.

Note: If someone uses a lot of words with negative connotation in their speech and constantly comes up with disparaging and negative comments, he/ she is likely to have a negative outlook about life and is quite likely to talk negative to himself/ herself and others around too. On the other hand, if someone has a positive language and uses positive words such as 'Yes, that can be done' or 'One should keep on trying', he/ she is likely to be an optimistic person who does not lose hope.

Discovering Personality

Personality often reflects through a person's social skills. Its study is in a branch of psychology called personality psychology. It relates to analyzing the unique characteristics that make a person an individual: it examines how people behave, how they experience feelings, how they think, how they express emotions.

Fundamentally, personality is the individual differences in the way people think, feel, and behave. When reading people, it is very crucial that you understand their personality because this understanding helps you correctly interpret their verbal and non-verbal language. This way, you can judge them according to who they are as different individuals could use one language to communicate different things.

Our personalities make us different: no two people see things in the exact same way. People have different communication styles and this, if not understood, may cause conflict. Understanding people's personalities, why they do, and say the things they do is not easy.

Below is an explanation of the major personality traits that encompass all personality types: the things that make people different according to the personality inventory called Myers-Briggs Type Indicator (MBTI).

Information Gathering: Sensing Versus Intuition

Sensing

Sensing: they are more practical. They rely on facts, numbers, and specific details to draw conclusions. They live in the present and care more about the problem at hand.

When talking to this kind of person about ideas, he or she may show interest because such a person wants facts and workable plan.

Intuition

They are insightful and inspirational. They find it easier to work with insights and theories. They are also future oriented.

This kind of person would be interested in discussing creative ideas.

Decision Making: Thinking Versus Feeling

The thinking

The thinkers are cold and impersonal. Their main motivation is logic and rational beginnings. They use logical analysis and objective methodologies to solve problems and make decisions.

The feeling

They are motivated by feelings to make decisions. They are more probable to show sympathy, concern, and support for others. They are more likely to depend on gut feeling, values, and their likes/dislikes to solve problems and make decisions.

Information Structuring: Judging Versus Perceiving

The judging

These ones like to make plans and stick with them: they are orderly. They are also task-oriented and purse things to the end.

The perceiving

They are spontaneous and rarely work with a plan. They want to stay open and are usually not very committed.

Relating to Others and the World: Extraversion versus Introversion

Extraversion

People with this trait draw energy from the outside world: it is their motivation factor. They have numerous contacts with other people and work well with others.

Introversion

Those with this trait tend to find comfort reflecting on their own perceptions, feelings, and thoughts. Their motivation comes from things in their inner world. They are unlikely to have numerous contacts. When interacting with others, they may seem not to be interested: they mean well; this is just their personality.

Putting It All Together: Analysing A Real Person

The previous chapters of this book have discussed at length the various theories and concepts used in psychology to understand different personalities. In order to make this information as practical as possible, it is vital that I provide you with a blueprint, a set of steps that you can use to better profile a person.

How do you apply the knowledge that you have just acquired in a real world scenario? What happens when you meet someone and you want to know what he or she is thinking? How do you know if they are lying or they are being truthful? How do you know if they like or they outright just resent you? Information like that would be priceless and this is what this chapter will focus on.

Think of it as the ultimate mind reader system. I believe that by relying on the steps outlined in this section of the book, you will be in a much better position to read and understand almost any person you may come across.

You will also be able to know yourself better and the information that you divulge to other people. No more living in the dark. No more embarrassing scenarios that could have been easily avoided. You are stepping into the light now. So let's get started.

Step 1: Start by reading what their body language says

Remember when I said in the first chapter of this book, that people communicate more with their body language than any other thing. If you want to become a proficient mind reader, this is your starting point.

1. Look at their outward appearance. What do you notice? Do they look flashy or are they casually dressed? Are their clothes seductive in a way? Seductive clothes may indicate sexual interest. Things like a cross may depict a person of high spiritual standards.

2. What posture do they have? Do they hold their head high as they walk or do they look down and cower? The former may be an indicator of high confidence while the latter is an indication of low confidence and self-esteem. A raised chest may indicate an egocentric person.

3. Watch for the look on their faces. Many times emotions are written clearly on people's faces. If you see a frown on someone's face, it may be likely that he or she is worried and deeply frustrated. Crow's feet, which are wrinkles around the eyes while smiling, are a sign of joy. A tense person may have clenched jaws. If the lips are pursed, it may be that the person is angry or bitter.

4. Look at the distance they keep. Is the person generally leaning towards or away from you? Leaning towards you may be a sign of interest in you. Also, if they keep a huge distance, that may be a sign that they either don't like you or they are afraid of you.

5. Look at their arms and legs. Are they crossed? Crossed arms and legs denote defensiveness or anger. If the legs are crossed, what direction is the top leg pointing towards. Most times, someone will point the legs towards someone he or she is most comfortable with.

6. What is the position of their hands? Are they holding their hands behind their backs? Are their hands in their pockets or in their laps? Are they at ease? Hidden hands are a suggestion that something is being hidden.

7. Are they biting their lips or nails? This is a sign that they are in a pressuring situation, which they are trying to ease themselves from.

Step 2: Make use of your intuition

Your intuition is simply your gut feeling. It is the information that you get through what your body feels instead of plain logic.

1. The first moment you meet someone, there is that quick reaction that occurs in your body before you even think of something else. This is what you need to pay attention to the most because it is the easiest to miss. This feeling will instantly tell you whether you are at ease with someone or not. It instinctively tells you whether a person can be trusted or not and many times it is always right.

2. You can also rely on your Goosebumps. This is normally a tingling feeling you get in your body whenever something happens. It can also happen when you experience a moment or meet with someone you think you may have met with before even though it may not be the case. It will easily tell you whether you are at ease with someone or something is amiss. It is often a good pointer that you can rely on.

3. People's physical symptoms may also show up in you in what psychologists call intuitive empathy. For instance, you may be sitting next to a person when all of a sudden, you start experiencing a headache or start feeling confused. If this is something you did not feel before, you may try asking the person. Chances could be that they are feeling the same and it is just your intuitive empathy at work. Such is the power of relying on your intuition.

4. Sometimes, your mind may receive a flash of insight. For instance, as you talk to someone, a thought may go through your mind. It typically happens so quickly that you may very easily miss it.

Step 3: Take not of the energy a person gives out

Another powerful way to understand a person may be through evaluating the energy they give out otherwise known as vibe. This can also be felt by intuition although some aspects of it can be observed physically.

1. As you get close to a person, try to get a feel of what their presence inspires in you. You could ask yourself questions like, "Do I get this friendly feeling that makes me want to be around this person more?" "Do I get this weird feeling of staying away from this person?" Asking yourself questions like these can help you determine what kind of energy a person is emitting.

2. Look into the person's eyes. Many times the eyes can give off very useful information about a person. Eyes can indicate whether someone could be lying, attracted, thinking deeply or even shy and insecure. Therefore, look into the eyes taking care not stare for too long. Ask yourself questions like, "Are the pupils dilating?" "Is he/she avoiding eye contact?" "Are the eyes looking to the left or to the right?" "How are the eyebrows behaving?" "Is he or she blinking a lot?"

3. Dilating pupils could be a sign of attraction. Eyes that are avoiding contact could be an indicator that either the person is lying about something or they are simply shy or nervous. This depends on the situation you may be dealing with. Eyes looking to the right could be a sign of creative thinking while looking to the left could indicate that a person could be trying to remember something. Blinking a lot could be a sign that they are flirting.

4. Observe how it feels when you shake hands or exchange a hug. Does the energy they emit feel comfortable and warm or does it feel negative and repelling? Do their hands feel sweaty? This could mean that they are overly anxious. Do they feel loose? This could indicate that the person is not confident.

5. Measure their tone when they speak or even laugh. How is the tone? Does it have a tinge of anger? Does it sound condescending? Does it sound whiny? Many times the tone of the voice is an indication of a person's rtue feeling at the moment or their nature. For instance, a condescending tone could indicate that a person is used to feeling the need to always feel superior.

I Need Your Help...

Thank you again for buying this book!

I hope this book was able to help you to get to know how to analyze people.

The next step is to use these techniques and you will be able to analyze whoever you want to.

Thanks to the development of psychology, we can now understand ourselves as well as the people around us. However, when it comes to behavior and language, we need to embrace the fact that there is no 'one size fits all'. We should try to understand people's personalities and environment before making conclusions.

If you found the book valuable, can you recommend it to others? One way to do that is to post a review on Amazon.

I want to reach as many people as I can with this book, and more reviews will help me accomplish that!

Thank you and good luck!

Preview Of "Habits Of Highly Effective People: The Power Of Habits: How Habits Influence Success"

Ponder over these questions:

What do you habitually think of first when you wake up? What do you do first thing in the morning as you get out of bed when you are still shaking off the cobwebs of that sweet, morning sleep? Do you dreamily make your way to the toilet, or before sitting down on the toilet seat, do you reach for your toothbrush and brush your teeth as you do your business? What do you do?

Pay special attention to your answers to these questions because as you will come to notice, habits are essentially things you do without much thought or consideration.

Defining Habits

In his book, *The Story of Philosophy: The Lives and Opinions of the World's Greatest Philosophers*, Will Durant, one of America's greatest writers, historians, and philosophers best known for, in collaboration with his wife, creating 11 volumes of the story of civilization, a groundbreaking piece of work that helped popularize philosophy, said:

"We are what we repeatedly do. Excellence, then, is not an act, but a habit."

This is the best description of habits: habits are things we repeatedly do. In retrospect, Will's quote is also the best show of how habits influence our every day life.

If you plop down onto your couch each evening after work, and you do this every day, this is your habit. If when your alarm beeps to signal your wake up time, instead of getting out of bed, you hit the snooze button, and you do this day in day out, this is a habit. At the core of habits is automation: *when something becomes a habit, you no longer use conscious effort to engage in it: you simply do.*

Going back to the questions in the first part of this section, what do you do first thing in the morning? If you wake up and make your way to the loo, do you use any mental effort? The answer is no; the reason behind this is because you have made your way to the loo in the morning so many times that your brain has created an automatic program for this behavior. The same applies to an idea such as exercising or meditating at a specific time of day every day.

Now that we have defined habits—*habits are things we do so repeatedly that they become automatic*—let us consider how habits affect our lives.

How Habits Influence Our Lives And Success

As you may have derived from our previous discussion, because habits are things we do repeatedly, naturally, we have good and bad habits that have various effects on our lives.

To expound on, and illustrate this, let us go back and use our earlier example where immediately after getting home from work, you plop down into the comforting embrace of your couch, and remote in hand, proceed to watch hours of your favorite TV show. 2 or 3 hours later, you reach for the phone, order take-out, sink back into your couch, and proceed to gobble down the pizza or whatever take-out you fancy as you watch TV into the wee hours of the morning. You do this every day.

In this scenario, what do you think most likely: you have a lean, fit body and your life is a success-laden story, or you epitomize the modern day American who wages a constant battle with excess weight, lack of success or progress, and struggles with effectiveness or time management: which do you think most probable? The latter is likely to be your case because of one simple thing: *you have bad habits.*

On the other hand, consider a scenario where after getting home from work, instead of gluing your butt to your super comfortable couch, you head straight into your bedroom, take off the day's clothes, get into your gym clothes, and proceed to engage in any form of exercise.

After this, you shower, plan and compartmentalize your work for the following day. You then read an inspirational book or the bible, follow this up with something that increases your value as a valued member of your workplace or society in general, and after, proceed to make (or order) a healthy meal.

In this scenario, what do you think most probable: that you have a healthy mind and body and successful in every area of your life, or that you are overweight and struggling to achieve semblances of success? The former is likely to be true. That is how habits affect your life.

When you adopt good positive habits that propel you towards the success you desire, habits such as exercising, reading, or personal development, you become highly successful in every area of your life. These hypotheticals vividly paint a picture of how habits influence our lives.

If your life is a series of bad habits (remember: habits define who we are), habits such as procrastination, lack of exercise, negative thinking (yes, negative thinking is habitual), consuming junk, and failing to plan, among others, you are likely to struggle with achieving any sort of success in your life.

On the other hand, if your life is a series of good habits, good habits such as the ones we described above such as meditation, self-improvement, exercise, healthy eating, etc.– you can bet success will come to you as easily as breathing: effortlessly.

To achieve success, therefore, you have to practice success habits, not just for one day, but repeatedly until that thing (activity) becomes habitual and automatic. Unfortunately, while this process seems such an easy one, at least on paper, the process of habit adoption or change is never an easy one.

To help you understand how to create new habits, break bad old habits, and replace them with new positive ones that drive you towards the success you crave, let us discuss the process of habit formation.

Check out the rest of Habits Of Highly Effective People on Amazon, go to: http://amzn.to/2qF5chr

Check Out My Other Books

Below you'll find some of my other popular books that are popular on Amazon and Kindle as well.

Alternatively, you can visit my author page on Amazon to see other work done by me.

Ketogenic Cookbook: Quick Low Calorie Ketogenic Crockpot Recipes with 7 Days Meal Plan

Freedom: How to Make Money Online and Become Financially Free by Creating Passive Income

Mediterranean Diet: Instant Pot Cookbook with Delicious Recipes

Alice the Superbug

Madison and Astrid's first magical journey

Intermittent Fasting: The Essential Beginners Guide for Women for Weight Loss

Chakra Healing: Chakra Healing and Karmic Awareness for Beginners

SEO 2017 for Growth: The Ultimate Guide to Learn Search Engine Optimization with Internet Marketing Tips

Psychology: How to Analyze People Using Human Psychological Techniques, Body Language Signals, Social Skills and Personality Types

Paleo Smoothies: Recipes to Energize and for Ultimate Health and Weight Loss

Belly Diet Smoothies: Delicious Smoothie Recipes to Flatten Your Belly, Improve Your Gut & Burn Fat

Keto Diet: Keto Diet Guide Cookbook for Beginners with Meal Plan and Simple, Delicious Recipes to Lose Weight and Look Good

Online Business from Scratch: The 9 Step Guide to Building a Profitable and Sustainable Online Business

Weight Loss: 20 Easy And Fast Diet Tips For Losing Weight - An Easy-To-Follow Weight Loss Guide

Ketogenic Cookbook: Ketogenic Cookbook for Beginners with 7 Days Meal Plan

Negative Calorie Diet: Cookbook & Guide Which Will Help You To Burn Body Fat, Lose Weight And Live Healthy

Negative Calorie Diet with Anti-Inflammatory Diet Guide

Make Money Online To Achieve Freedom

Negative Calorie Diet with Smart Fat Guide

Negative Calorie Diet & Clean Eating: Cookbook & Guide Which Will Help You To Burn Body Fat, Lose Weight And Live Healthy

Smart Fat: Cookbook with Fat Meals Which Help You to Lose Weight, Get Healthy and Improve Brain Function

Anti-Inflammatory Diet Guide: The Guide to Reduce Inflammation and Live a Healthy Life Without Pain

Essential Oils: The Young Living Book Guide of Natural Remedies for Beginners for Pets, For Dogs

Clean Eating: Cookbook and Guide to Restore Your Body's Natural Balance and Eat Healthy

Anti-Inflammatory Diet Guide: The Guide to Reduce Inflammation and Live a Healthy Life Without Pain

Dash Diet: Cookbook for Weight Loss with Action Plan and Easy Recipes

Air Fryer Cookbook: Quick, Healthy and Easy Low Carb Air Fryer Recipes

Psychology & Habits Of Highly Effective People Box Set

Leptin Resistance: Leptin Diet to Control Your Hormones, Get Permanent Weight Loss, Cure Obesity and Live Healthy

Negative Calorie Diet & Dash Diet Box Set

Negative Calorie Diet & Weight Loss Box Set

Habits of Highly Effective People: What Are the Habits of Successful People?

Slow Cooker: Cookbook with Slow Cooker Recipes

Weight Loss Cookbook: Meal Prep Cookbook for Weight Loss and Clean Eating

Weight Loss Cookbook: Mediterranean Diet for Lasting Weight Loss

Negative Calorie Diet & Dash Diet Box Set

Slow Cooker & Instant Pot Box Set

Children Books: Madison and Astrid's first magical journey & Alice the Superbug Box Set

Belly Diet: The Zero Belly Diet Step-By-Step Guide Which Helps You to Lose Your Belly and Enjoy Your Flat Belly

Weight Loss: 20 Easy and Fast Diet Tips for Losing Weight - An Easy-To-Follow Weight Loss Guide

Instant Pot: Instant Pot Pressure Cooker Cookbook with Easy and Healthy Recipes

Vegan Cookbook: Vegan Cookbook For Beginners, For Kids And For Teens For Diabetics With Pictures

Low Carb: Low Carb Diet Cookbook with Low Carb Keto Recipes for Batch Cooking

Ketogenic Cooking: Ketogenic Cooking With Your Instant Pot

Passive Income: Passive Income Tutorial with 7 Online Ideas to Generate Passive Income Streams for Beginners

Low Carb Diet: Low Carb Diet Recipes Cookbook for Beginners for Batch Cooking

Make Money from Home: How to Make Money Online and Escape the 9-5 Rat Race

Amazon Customer Service

Kindle Unlimited

Bonus: Free Personalized Quiz & Report

When you subscribe to Freedom Destination via email, you will get free access to an ebook. All you have to do is enter your email address to get instant access.

In this quick quiz, you will find out exactly what is energetically holding you back from attracting all of the prosperity, love, happiness and abundance that you desire, PLUS receive:

- A FREE personalized quiz assessment

- A FREE video that teaches you the secret to unlocking your powers of abundance

To get instant access to these incredible personalized quiz, go to: http://bit.ly/2sOWmQH